US BORDERS

CROSSING THE BORDER

CATHLEEN SMALL

LUCENT
P R E S S

Published in 2018 by
Lucent Press, an Imprint of Greenhaven Publishing, LLC
353 3rd Avenue
Suite 255
New York, NY 10010

Produced for Lucent by Calcium
Designer: Jeni Child
Picture researcher: Rachel Blount
Editors: Sarah Eason and Nancy Dickmann

Picture credits: Cover: Shutterstock: Vinokurov Kirill (top), Peter Titmuss (main); Inside: Shutterstock: Orhan Cam 50, Richard Cavalleri 34, Sylvie Corriveau 47, CPQ 16–17, Diego G Diaz 61, Doublex 48, Everett Historical 35, 36–37, 38, 40, 43, Zack Frank 13, Martin Froyda 10, Jason and Bonnie Grower 57t, A Katz 32, Radoslaw Lecyk 39, Rainer Lesniewski 18, 57b, Marla Margarla 4, Philip Pilosian 27, 31, Michael Rosebrock 58–59, Dan Schreiber 21, Mark Van Scyoc 33, Sherwood 55, Alan Smillie 44–45, Sherry V Smith 5, Joseph Sohm 53, Spatuletail 9, James Steidl 60, Reinhard Tiburzy 19, Peter Titmuss 46, Tupungato 24, Volina 14, Jiri Vondrous 51, Sam Wagner 22, Wildnerdpix 8, Leonard Zhukovsky 29; U.S. Customs & Border Protection: Donna Burton 26; Wikimedia Commons: Donna Burton 12, Ad Meskens 15, Erik Oberg/Island Conservation 49, Police 28, Dan Sorensen 11, The United States government 7, UpstateNYer 6, John Yu/Connie Young Yu 42.

Cataloging-in-Publication Data

Names: Small, Cathleen.
Title: U.S. borders / Cathleen Small.
Description: New York : Lucent Press, 2018. | Series: Crossing the border | Includes index.
Identifiers: ISBN 9781534562509 (library bound) | ISBN 9781534562516 (ebook) | ISBN 9781534562813 (paperback)
Subjects: LCSH: Border security--United States--Juvenile literature. | National security--Law and legislation--United States--Juvenile literature. | United States--Emigration and immigration--Juvenile literature.
Classification: LCC JV6483.S63 2018 | DDC 363.28'50973--dc23

CPSIA compliance information: Batch #CW18KL: For further information contact Greenhaven Publishing LLC, New York, New York at 1-844-317-7404.

Please visit our website, www.greenhavenpublishing.com. For a free color catalog of all our high-quality books, call toll free 1-844-317-7404 or fax 1-844-317-7405.

CROSSING THE BORDER

RO453633173

CONTENTS

CHAPTER 1

THE UNITED STATES-MEXICO BORDER

The United States has two main international land borders—one with Canada and one with Mexico. The border with Canada is actually longer than the border with Mexico, but the Mexican border is more heavily traveled and is definitely the more controversial as far as immigration is concerned.

UNITED STATES-MEXICO BORDER GEOGRAPHY

While the United States–Mexico border is heavily traveled, it's actually not that long when compared to the entire length of the United States. From east to west, the United States is about 2,800 miles (4,506 km) across, not counting Alaska and Hawaii. The mileage varies slightly depending on which cities are used as endpoints. The United States' southern international border, with Mexico, is only 1,989 miles (3,201 km). That's a long distance, but it's only about two-thirds the width of the entire United States.

The United States lies between the countries of Canada and Mexico in the continent of North America.

The United States–Mexico border starts in the west at the Pacific Ocean, just south of San Diego, California. It then travels along the southern edges of California, Arizona, and New Mexico before reaching El Paso, Texas, at the western edge of the state. From there, the border follows the Rio Grande in a mostly southwest direction along the bottom edge of Texas. It ends at the Gulf of Mexico, just east of Brownsville, Texas. By far, the longest portion of the border on the United States side is through Texas, and the shortest is through California.

On the Mexico side, the border runs along the northern edges of six Mexican states. From west to east, they are Baja California, Sonora, Chihuahua, Coahuila, Nuevo León, and Tamaulipas. In the Mexican states, the longest stretch of border runs through Chihuahua, and the shortest is through Nuevo León.

BORDER CROSSINGS

People must cross the border between the two countries at an official border crossing point. There are a total of 48 border crossings along the United States–Mexico border, with a total of 330 ports of entry. This breaks down to four main crossing points in California, six in Arizona, two in New Mexico, and twelve in Texas. Each of these main border crossings can have multiple crossing points. They might include roads for cars and other vehicles, walkways for pedestrians, railroads for trains, and ferries for water crossings.

At Border Field State Park beach in San Diego, a wall extends out into the ocean to separate the United States from Mexico.

THE BUSIEST BORDER CROSSING

California actually has the shortest shared border with Mexico of any of the four U.S. states that border it. And California borders only one Mexican state (Baja California), while the other three states all border at least two. But nevertheless, the busiest border crossing on the United States–Mexico border happens to fall in California. It's called the San Ysidro Port of Entry, and it goes between San Diego, California, and Tijuana, Mexico. An average of about 40,000 vehicles cross from Tijuana to San Diego each day, along with about 19,000 pedestrians. And that is just the people crossing the border into the United States.

Part of the reason this crossing is so busy is that many Mexicans living in Tijuana are legally employed in San Diego. And some Americans live in the nearby Mexican towns of Tijuana, Rosarito Beach, and Ensenada. They commute into the United States each day for school or work.

Northbound traffic waits to enter San Ysidro, California.

History of the Border

The Mexican territory used to extend farther into the United States than it does now. The region was originally controlled by the Spanish, who called it the Kingdom of New Spain. In the early 1800s the United States completed the Louisiana Purchase, in which it bought a huge area of land west of the Mississippi River from France. Settlers soon began to move to this new region. Shortly thereafter, Mexico gained its independence from Spain and began to try to establish a northern border.

By 1842, Mexico had established its current territory, but it also expanded far north of where it ends today. Most of California, Arizona, and New Mexico were part of Mexico, along with parts of Nevada, Colorado, Kansas, Wyoming, Oklahoma, and Utah. The Mexican government had tried to establish a population in what is now Texas, but Texas declared independence in 1836. It was later annexed by the United States in 1845.

The Mexican–American war broke out in 1846 and lasted until 1848. The Treaty of Guadalupe Hidalgo, signed on February 2, 1848, ended the war and established the Rio Grande as the border between the United States and Mexico. The United States had already annexed Texas by that point, but the Treaty of Guadalupe Hidalgo also gave California to the United States, as well as parts of New Mexico, Arizona, Nevada, Utah, Wyoming, and Colorado.

Before the states were divided as they are today, part of the United States was split into territories.

A MOVING BORDER

It would seem that choosing a river as a border would be a simple way of marking out territory. After all, the river has existed for thousands of years. It's also an obvious geographical marker—one side of the river belongs to the United States, and the other side belongs to Mexico. It's relatively easy to patrol, too. No need to build a fence to show where the border is and keep people from crossing illegally—Border Patrol agents simply need to patrol the riverfront areas.

However, there is one small problem: rivers don't stay in the exact same place all the time. The Rio Grande has actually shifted south over the years. A flood in 1864 made a fairly large shift in the river, for example. By 1873, it became apparent that the southward-shifting river had resulted in the United States gaining approximately 600 acres (243 hectares) of Mexican territory, just south of the Texas border. It took nearly 100 years, but in 1963 the United States and Mexico negotiated a border treaty, and Mexico regained most of the land it had lost.

Immigrants can cross the Rio Grande on simple boats like this one.

COMPLETING THE BORDER

The border between the two countries was not complete until the Gadsden Purchase was negotiated in 1853. This purchase was designed to allow the United States to expand the Transcontinental Railroad to the deep southern part of the west, but it also finalized the United States–Mexico border in southern Arizona and part of southern New Mexico.

The Treaty of Guadalupe Hidalgo and the Gadsden Purchase show how some of the border towns came to be. When the Treaty of Guadalupe Hidalgo was signed, Mexicans living in the areas that had been annexed to the United States were offered the chance to stay in the United States if they pledged loyalty to the United States government. More than 90 percent of these people chose to do so, resulting in fairly heavy Mexican settlement in the new United States territories that had previously been part of Mexico.

On the other hand, when the Gadsden Purchase was signed, Mexicans were encouraged to move south, out of the United States and into the land along the northern border of Mexico. They were given free land in that area so that they could help repopulate the area at the Mexican border.

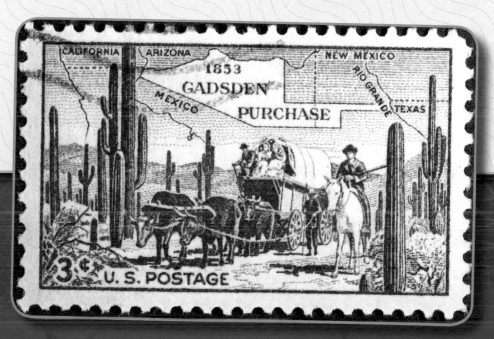

 The Gadsden Purchase was commemorated on a postage stamp.

BORDER TERRAIN

Due to the United States–Mexico border spanning more than 1,900 miles (3,058 km), the terrain around it is varied. Near San Diego, at its westernmost point, the border crossing is a relatively temperate climate, being located fairly near the ocean. However, as the border stretches east, the terrain becomes more hostile. In the eastern part of California and in Arizona and New Mexico, the terrain is largely desert near the border. Summers are brutally hot, while winters are generally mild and pleasant. At any time of year (but particularly during the summer), heavy rains in the sun-baked desert can cause flash flooding.

Because of these differences, there are large portions of the border that are not as heavily patrolled as others. In the desert, people are less likely to attempt illegal crossings, because they know the harsh conditions can be deadly. These areas are often lightly populated, which means a dehydrated person in the desert stands little chance of finding help if he or she needs it.

 A small but sturdy steel fence marks the border between the United States and Mexico in Arizona's Tinajas Altas mountains.

THE MIGRANTS OF EL CAMINO DEL DIABLO

The Sonoran Desert runs through northern Mexico and southern Arizona and California. It is lightly patrolled by Border Patrol agents because the conditions are so harsh that there is little chance of immigrants making it across. The deadliest crossing is known as El Camino del Diablo (meaning "Devil's Highway"), and it runs from the Mexican border town of Sonoyta to Ajo, Arizona, 30 miles (48 km) inside the United States border. Heat, lack of water, and deadly animals such as scorpions and rattlesnakes make it extremely dangerous. In the last five years, more than 1,400 immigrants have died on the trail.

Jose Mendoza was a Mexican citizen who could not support his wife and six children on what he earned in Mexico. He paid a smuggler $600 to help him navigate El Camino del Diablo and make it into the United States. They set out on an August night, in temperatures of 100° F (38° C), without enough water or food. They walked for hours and then stopped to rest. By the light of day, the temperature rose to 120° F (49° C), and they had already drunk all their water.

Their lives were saved when they found a water station that a church group had put out in the desert. Without it, Mendoza might have ended up like fellow immigrant Lizbet Hernandez, who died during a crossing on the same night.

The forbidding terrain of El Camino del Diablo is surveyed by Border Patrol agents in helicopters.

11

THE RIO GRANDE

Going into Texas, the border follows the Rio Grande. In some ways, this is a more forgiving climate than the desert. There's water, farmland, and more people around. At some points the Rio Grande is relatively easy to cross on a raft, because the water runs slowly. But at other points, it can be deadly. The river has strong undercurrents, which can be deadly for even strong swimmers. There are whirlpools hiding under some parts of the seemingly calm water. Branches and sharp rocks make potentially deadly obstacles. In addition, parts of the riverbed are lined with a sticky slime that can trap a swimmer's foot. The Border Patrol has documented 6,023 deaths from October 2000 through September 2016 of immigrants trying to illegally cross the southwestern border of the United States.

This part of the border is often more heavily patrolled. U.S. Immigration and Customs Enforcement and Border Patrol agents know that many immigrants will try to cross, so they keep a close eye on the American side of the river. Some of the immigrants who try to cross are aware of this but don't care—they climb out of the river and walk right up to Border Patrol agents, asking to be granted asylum. They know they'll be put in detention centers while their background checks are done and their request for asylum is evaluated. They feel that being essentially imprisoned is worth it for the chance to gain the legal right to stay in the United States.

Federal agents patrol the Rio Grande in Texas by boat.

 The Rio Grande flows through Big Bend National Park as it passes through Texas.

 ## ORBIN'S EXPERIENCE

PERSONAL STORIES

Orbin was a 15-year-old boy from Honduras, one of many Central American immigrants who attempt to enter the United States by crossing the Rio Grande. Like many from Central America, Orbin was fleeing violence.

Orbin didn't know his father, and his mother had left Honduras when Orbin was six years old. Orbin stayed with family, but he made the decision to leave Honduras when he saw gang members beat his best friend to death for refusing to join the gang. They threatened to kill Orbin, too, if he didn't join within a month.

Orbin didn't doubt their threats. His uncle gave him some money, and Orbin spent the next few weeks moving through Honduras, Guatemala, and Mexico until he reached the Rio Grande. He was frightened to cross the river, but he did it—because the prospect of going back to Honduras and being killed was worse. As a strong swimmer, Orbin was lucky enough to make it across.

CHAPTER 2

THE UNITED STATES–CANADA BORDER

The border between the United States and Canada isn't just the longest international border in the United States, it's the longest international border between two countries in the world. However, it does not get the same attention as the United States–Mexico border, most likely because it's not nearly as heavily crossed by undocumented immigrants.

 The Canadian border is by far the United States' longest international border, especially when you include the Alaskan border.

The United States is the world's fourth largest country in area, and Canada is the second largest country in area. For the most part, Canada sits snugly on top of the northern border of the United States, almost like a hat. If you can picture a feather in that cap, that would be Alaska—part of the United States, even though it's technically attached to the far western end of Canada, rather than to the rest of the contiguous United States.

Border Geography

Because of this geography, the United States–Canada border is extremely long. It is actually nearly twice as long as the United States is wide. This is because the border does not follow a straight line—in some places it follows waterways. The total length of the United States–Canada border is 5,525 miles (8,892 km), and Canada's border with Alaska makes up 1,538

The Thousand Islands Bridge connects the United States to Ontario.

miles (2,475 km) of that. The Alaska–Canada portion of the border is the longest segment. The Pennsylvania–Canada portion is the shortest segment, at just 42 miles (68 km).

The United States–Canada border spans 13 U.S. states. Traveling from west to east, they are Alaska, Washington, Idaho, Montana, North Dakota, Minnesota, Michigan, Ohio, Pennsylvania, New York, Vermont, New Hampshire, and Maine. Given that the United States is made up of 50 states, that means more than a quarter of the U.S. states share a border with Canada.

On the Canadian side, the border touches the southern part of eight Canadian provinces. From west to east, they are Yukon, British Columbia, Alberta, Saskatchewan, Manitoba, Ontario, Quebec, and New Brunswick.

Crossing Points

The United States–Canada border is so long that there are many ports of entry and border crossings. There are several notable crossings, though. For example, the Ambassador Bridge crossing between Detroit, Michigan, and Ontario, Canada, is the busiest commercial crossing. There are also major crossings between Vancouver, Canada, and northern Washington; between Ontario, Canada, and Buffalo, New York; and between Ontario, Canada, and Port Huron, Michigan.

A MOST BEAUTIFUL BORDER

Just like the United States–Mexico border is partly formed by the Rio Grande, the United States–Canada border also has a river making up part of it: the Niagara River. It flows north from Lake Erie to Lake Ontario. Like the Rio Grande, it is known for its great natural beauty.

Both rivers also form a substantial obstacle to anyone wanting to cross the border. The Rio Grande is notorious for being a deadly crossing that claims many lives. The Niagara River is dangerous too, but it kills far fewer immigrants because no one attempts to swim across it. It is a wide, fast-moving river that would be impossible to cross safely. And it also contains Niagara Falls, a deadly but stunning waterfall. Anyone attempting to cross the river near the falls would likely be swept over what is the most powerful waterfall in North America.

Although it's not a feasible crossing, it is a stunning tourist attraction. In fact, it has been a popular honeymoon destination for years. Niagara Falls is actually made up of three waterfalls. Both Bridal Veil Falls and the American Falls are entirely on the United States side of the river. Horseshoe Falls, though, the section that is most often photographed, is on both the American and Canadian sides.

Only a small part of Horseshoe Falls lies within the United States. The rest is in Canada.

HISTORY OF THE BORDER

Given that the United States formed over many decades, it's not surprising that the United States–Canada border has also had a long and somewhat complicated history. When the first settlers came to the United States in the 1600s, they mainly settled in the east. Over the years, the population expanded westward, and more and more territories were annexed to the United States. Along with that came the formalizing of the border with Canada.

In 1783, the Treaty of Paris established part of the border between the eastern United States and what was then known as British North America. This portion was at the southern edge of Quebec in Canada and formed the northern borders of Vermont and part of New York. However, some errors in surveying and disputes about land claims meant that this portion of the border was redefined in 1842, as part of the Webster–Ashburton Treaty. This treaty redefined the border between Canada and New Hampshire, Vermont, and New York.

Natural Borders

Just like the Rio Grande made a natural border between Mexico and Texas, the St. Lawrence River and the Great Lakes helped form a natural border between what is now Ontario and parts of the United States. The border established at this point ended roughly at Lake of the Woods, in Minnesota.

The Webster–Ashburton Treaty, which had redefined the borders of some northeastern states, also redefined part of the border between what is now Ontario and Minnesota.

The Great Lakes and the St. Lawrence River help define the border between Canada and the United States.

Westward Expansion

As the United States' expansion westward continued, so did the westward expansion of British North America. The Treaty of 1818 extended the border to roughly the Rocky Mountains, along the 49th parallel. The United States gave up some land at the northern part of the Louisiana Purchase to British North America, and in return British North America gave up some land in Minnesota and North Dakota's Red River Valley to the United States.

In 1844, the United States and the United Kingdom (which controlled the Province of Canada at that point) had a dispute over how the United States–Canada border should be defined in the Rocky Mountain region. The Oregon Treaty of 1846 settled the dispute and set the border at the 49th parallel. It had already been set at the 49th parallel in 1818, but the United States had wanted to change it to roughly the 54th parallel.

Some parts of the border, such as this spot near Skagway, Alaska, are quite unassuming.

BORDER CHANGES

The western border around Washington and British Columbia was tricky because it involved a lot of waterways and islands. That border was not solidified until 1872. The Alaska–Canada border was also a bit tricky to define, since Alaska was part of the United States but was not attached to the United States geographically. That boundary was finally determined in 1903, after a tribunal involving the United States, Canada, and the United Kingdom.

In 1908, the United States and United Kingdom signed a treaty that, among other things, called for the borders to be resurveyed along the St. Lawrence River and the Great Lakes. This resulted in some minor changes to the United States–Canada border.

MAPPING BORDERS

Since borders can shift (as in the case of the Rio Grande), in 1925 the International Boundary Commission was established, involving commissioners from both Canada and the United States. Part of the Commission's purpose is to survey and map the border, maintain border markers, and keep the border clear of brush.

CROSS-BORDER AIRPORTS

The United States–Canada border has one feature that the Mexico border does not: cross-border airports. These are airports that are on both U.S. and Canadian soil. They were built before World War II so that aircraft built in the United States could be legally transferred into Canada. At that time, Canada had entered the war, but the United States had not.

U.S. military pilots were not allowed to deliver aircraft into Canada by air. They could, however, fly the planes to an airport in the far north of the United States and then tow it over the border using tractors or horses. The easiest way to do this was to build cross-border airports. The six that were built still exist. They are Piney Pinecreek Border Airport, which straddles Manitoba and Minnesota; International Peace Garden Airport, which straddles Manitoba and North Dakota; Coronach/Scobey Border Station Airport, which straddles Saskatchewan and Montana; Coutts/ Ross International Airport, which straddles Alberta and Montana; Whetstone International Airport, which also straddles Alberta and Montana; and Avey Field State Airport, which straddles British Columbia and Washington.

BORDER TERRAIN

Because the United States–Canada border stretches so far, its terrain is quite varied. In some parts, such as at the Alaska–Canada border, it extends a long way north. In the summer, the weather is relatively mild and pleasant, and daylight hours are quite long. But in the winter, the border this far north is forbiddingly cold. Anyone attempting to cross illegally would be ill-advised to do it in the winter.

In the west, the border climate is relatively mild in the summer and cold in the winter—though not as harsh as it is farther north. Vancouver, British Columbia, a border city in the far western part of Canada, has tall mountains around it. Its American counterpart to the south, Seattle, Washington, does as well. But the actual United States–Canada border in that region is flat and reasonably unremarkable. It is different from the harsh desert climate of the border with Mexico in the Sonoran Desert.

Moving farther east, parts of the United States–Canada border are mountainous, dividing the Rocky Mountains in the United States and the Canadian Rockies in Canada. Summers are mild and winters are cold and snowy. There are also plains regions, near the Midwest in the United States. They can be extremely cold in the winter and hot and humid in the summer.

Glacier National Park spans the border, with some parts in Montana and others in British Columbia and Alberta.

WATER BORDERS

The Great Lakes region is known for brutally cold winters, and in some cases the border is in the middle of water, making crossing difficult if one were trying to do it illegally. Of course, there are bridges and tunnels to allow legal crossings. Where the border follows the St. Lawrence River, the climate stays similarly forbidding in the winter.

 Winters on Lake Superior in northern Minnesota can be absolutely frigid.

In short, if one were planning an illegal border crossing based on climate, winter would be the time to cross the United States–Mexico border, and summer would be the time to cross the United States–Canada border. While the border with Canada does not typically have venomous scorpions and rattlesnakes, the northern regions of the United States and the southern regions of Canada are home to some animals that can pose danger to humans, such as bears and wolves.

HEADING TO CANADA

Illegal border crossings between the United States and Canada aren't nearly as common as between Mexico and the United States. However, in late 2016 Canada experienced a spike in people crossing the border into Canada and asking for asylum. Just as there are parts of the United States–Mexico border that are unsecured, there are also parts of the United States–Canada border that are fairly easy to cross undetected.

One common route for people seeking asylum in Canada leads into Quebec. Families describe crossing a "little ditch" to walk from the United States into Canada. The 2016 total for people entering Quebec and requesting asylum was nearly five times as high as the 2015 total. The number of people doing so in November 2016 was higher than all of the people doing so for the entire year of 2015.

Some think the reason has to do with Donald Trump's election as president of the United States in November 2016. Trump loudly and publicly claimed that one of his goals as president would be to deport immigrants who were in the United States illegally. Canada is known to have a high rate of granting asylum, so families who feared deportation under the Trump administration may have begun sneaking over to Canada to seek asylum there. This theory is supported by the fact that many of the people walking into Quebec and requesting asylum are from Eritrea, Syria, Sudan, Yemen, and surrounding countries—many of which are countries Trump is attempting to enforce strict immigration laws for.

CHAPTER 3

U.S. IMMIGRATION AND BORDER AGENCIES

People can cross the United States–Mexico border and the United States–Canada border on foot or by vehicle, at various entry points. However, people can also enter the United States by boat and by airplane. This means that every international airport or seaport is also a potential entry point for immigrants, adding up to a huge number of different places and ways to enter the United States. Controlling and monitoring immigration in all of these areas is overseen by the Department of Homeland Security.

 Newark Liberty Airport in New Jersey is one of the busiest international airports in the United States.

THE UNITED STATES AND ITS TERRITORIES

Every citizen knows that the United States is made up of 50 states: the contiguous 48 states, plus Alaska and Hawaii. What is less well known is that the United States also has 16 territories. Eleven of these territories are small islands with no permanent residents, but five of them are permanently inhabited.

These five inhabited U.S. territories are Puerto Rico, Guam, the U.S. Virgin Islands, American Samoa, and the Northern Mariana Islands. Anyone born in Guam, Puerto Rico, the Northern Mariana Islands, and the U.S. Virgin Islands becomes a United States citizen at birth.

However, a person born in American Samoa is only a United States citizen if one of his or her parents was already an American citizen. If a person born in American Samoa has native Samoan parents, he or she is considered to be a U.S. national rather than a citizen, and must go through the naturalization process in order to become a U.S. citizen.

U.S. CUSTOMS AND BORDER PROTECTION

U.S. Customs and Border Protection (CBP) is part of the Department of Homeland Security, and it is the main entity responsible for handling immigration. It is considered a law-enforcement organization, and it has more than 60,000 employees, making it the largest federal law enforcement agency.

CBP handles customs, immigration, border security, and agricultural inspection. On any given day, CBP processes nearly one million people, of which some are immigrants and some are just visiting the United States. CBP also screens more than 67,000 cargo containers arriving by ship. Reportedly, of the one million people CBP screens each day, they arrest more than 1,100 individuals who are attempting to enter illegally. They also seize nearly 6 tons (5.4 mt) of illegal drugs each day.

THE FOUR-LEGGED EMPLOYEES OF CBP

More than 60,000 people work for CBP, but there are also four-legged employees working for the department. The CBP Canine Program was created in 2009, when two other canine-detection programs under CBP were merged. Drug-sniffing dogs had first been used by the U.S. Customs Service (the precursor of CBP) as long ago as 1970 to detect marijuana and hashish being smuggled over the borders. They quickly learned that the dogs could detect other drugs as well, and the program expanded. After September 11, 2001, CBP began to use dogs to detect explosives as well. In addition, some are trained to help with search and rescue operations. The dogs are currently stationed at more than 70 commercial ports and more than 70 Border Patrol stations in the United States.

A CBP officer and his canine assistant inspect vehicles coming into Texas from Mexico.

CBP STATIONS

Approximately two-thirds of CBP officers work at stations along the two major international U.S. borders. CBP officers are also stationed at airports with international flights and at ports where boats come from international waters. They do much of their agricultural inspection at the land and sea borders to make sure that no pests or disease are brought into the United States on infected agriculture.

INTERNATIONAL AIRPORTS

It's virtually impossible to know how many international airports exist in the United States. Some are obvious: they have "international" in their name, and they have scheduled international flights daily. But there are also smaller regional airports that have periodic flights to other countries, such as Canada. Technically, to be an international airport, the airfield needs only to have a U.S. Customs office. There are even small airstrips without air traffic control towers that have some level of customs service. For example, one small airstrip in the Florida Keys fits this description. Some small privately owned airstrips, such as one in Klamath Falls, Oregon, also have periodic customs service when needed.

 Los Angeles International Airport handles flights from all over the world.

OFFICE OF IMMIGRATION STATISTICS

While CBP handles the relatively visible part of immigration, there's another agency under the Department of Homeland Security that also works with immigration. The Office of Immigration Statistics (OIS) collects data about immigrants and shares it with the public and with Congress. This office also establishes reliability standards for the data it collects.

Collecting Data

OIS collects data about such groups as refugees and asylees, green card holders (also known as lawful permanent residents, or LPRs), nonimmigrants who were granted temporary admission to the United States, and more. They compile population estimates for all of these groups, and they also compile data about actions taken to prevent immigrants from entering the country illegally.

The goal of this data collection and sharing is to help the government evaluate the impacts of current immigration laws on demographics, economics, and environmental and social concerns. Immigration law and policy is always changing, and when it does, lawmakers consult the data compiled by OIS to determine the best course of action.

U.S. Immigration and Customs Enforcement

While OIS handles data and CBP handles the day-to-day processing of people, cargo, and agriculture entering the country, another agency under the Department of Homeland Security is charged with investigating and enforcing more than 400 federal laws related to immigration. This agency is known as U.S. Immigration and Customs Enforcement (ICE). CBP is considered a law-enforcement division of the Department of Homeland Security, while ICE is an investigative division.

Part of an ICE agent's job is to arrest immigrants who have violated laws or are subject to deportation.

ICE was formed when the Homeland Security Act of 2002 was passed. It was formed from a combination of several other smaller agencies, including the Immigration and Naturalization Service and the investigative employees of the U.S. Customs Service.

ICE RESPONSIBILITIES

ICE is much smaller than CBP. While CBP has more than 60,000 employees, ICE currently has roughly 20,000. It has two main divisions: Enforcement and Removal Operations, and Homeland Security Investigations. Under each of these divisions are several smaller divisions.

The Enforcement and Removal Operations division is responsible for enforcing immigration laws and deporting immigrants discovered to be living in the United States without documentation. They find these undocumented immigrants in a number of ways. Some are on teams to locate undocumented immigrants who have a Warrant of Deportation issued for them. Some locate undocumented immigrants who are in prison for breaking a U.S. law.

The Department of Homeland Security also provides protection and security at major public events.

Homeland Security Investigations, on the other hand, works on issues such as human trafficking and smuggling, drug and weapons trafficking, gangs, manufacturing and distribution of illegal identification documents, money laundering, and cybercrimes. If an issue is thought to threaten national security, then Homeland Security Investigations handles it. If it's a matter of locating and deporting undocumented immigrants, Enforcement and Removal Operations handles it.

MAURICIO

Mauricio was a 19-year-old undocumented immigrant living outside of Baltimore, Maryland, when he was taken into custody in 2016. He was heading to work at 7 a.m. when he was approached by six immigration officers, who searched his wallet and found a paper showing he had missed a court date. Due to the missed court date, they arrested him and put him in jail for 25 days. He was eventually released while waiting for a new court date. Immigration proceedings can take a long time, and while Mauricio waits for his, he lives in uncertainty about whether he will be allowed to stay.

Mauricio and his two brothers, Antonio and Miguel, want to become permanent residents of the United States. They grew up in a poverty-stricken family of 13 children living in Guatemala. Their father was murdered by a Guatemalan gang, right in front of Miguel, the boys' mother, and one of their sisters. The brothers want to live and work legally in the United States so they can send money back to the rest of their impoverished family still living in Guatemala. Whether their wish is granted remains to be seen and is in the hands of the immigration courts.

DETENTION CENTERS

Immigration and Customs Enforcement is also in charge of operating detention centers where undocumented immigrants are held while awaiting deportation. Some of the undocumented immigrants are also held in jails and prisons; between the three, there are about 31,000 undocumented immigrants held in detention at any given time. As some are deported, new ones arrive. This means there is a fairly steady population of undocumented immigrants awaiting transport back to their home country.

 The Metropolitan Detention Center in Los Angeles holds inmates before and during court proceedings.

PRESIDENT TRUMP, ICE, AND DEPORTATION

As of early 2017, ICE was slated to get a big increase in its number of immigration officers. Five days after taking office, President Donald Trump signed an executive order directing ICE to hire 10,000 additional immigration officers. At the time, there were only about 5,800 immigration officers employed by ICE, which means Trump's order would nearly triple the number of immigration officers available to find and deport undocumented immigrants. Trump's goal in this was to keep one of his campaign promises and increase the number of undocumented immigrants apprehended and deported from the United States.

DEPORTATION CONTROVERSY

Days after he won the presidential election in November 2016, Trump was interviewed on the television program *60 Minutes*. In the interview, he said that he planned to immediately deport 2 to 3 million undocumented immigrants with criminal records after he was inaugurated as president.

During his campaign, Donald Trump promised to make sweeping changes in immigration policy.

Illegal immigration was an issue that he had been talking about throughout his campaign. "When Mexico sends its people, they're not sending their best," he had said during his presidential campaign. "They're sending people that have lots of problems, and they're bringing those problems...They're bringing drugs. They're bringing crime.... And some, I assume, are good people."

DIVIDED OPINION

Not surprisingly, this comment brought a lot of controversy. Some people agreed with Trump that immigrants were bringing crime. At the same time, many others thought that Trump was making a bold and unfair stereotypical statement about immigrants.

Trump signed an executive order just days after taking office, which was the first step in his deportation plan. ICE followed up two weeks later by carrying out immigration raids in at least six U.S. states: New York, California, North and South Carolina, Georgia, and Illinois. There were reported raids in Florida, Kansas, Texas, and Virginia as well.

Past presidents, including Barack Obama, had authorized similar immigrant raids, but these raids targeted only undocumented immigrants who had broken laws. It was reported that during the raids shortly after Trump took office, law-abiding undocumented immigrants were also arrested and ordered for deportation.

AN UNCERTAIN FUTURE

It's not yet clear whether Trump will really be able to keep his promise to deport 2 to 3 million undocumented immigrants with criminal records. No matter how many immigration officials are hired, there may not actually be that many undocumented immigrants with criminal records for them to find.

It appears that the number Trump was basing his comment on was a number from a Department of Homeland Security report from 2013 that said there were 1.9 million "removable criminal aliens" living in the United States. That 1.9 million number does indeed include undocumented immigrants who have committed crimes—but it also includes people with green cards or temporary visas who have committed crimes. Whatever happens, ICE will certainly be gaining new immigration agents. How they will be put to work remains to be seen.

The Department of Homeland Security oversees numerous offices involved in immigration and deportation.

CHAPTER 4

IMMIGRATION ISLANDS

When thinking about historical immigration to the United States, two islands immediately jump to mind: one in the east and one in the west. In the early parts of the 20th century, Ellis Island and Angel Island saw more than 13 million immigrants step on their shores, hoping for admittance to the United States.

Ellis Island was once home to a fort, but it was later enlarged by reclaiming land from New York Bay.

THE GATEWAY TO THE EAST COAST

Ellis Island is one of the most famous islands in U.S. history. More than 12 million immigrants entered the United States through Ellis Island in the years from 1892 to 1954. Most people think of it as being part of New York, because it is located not far from the Statue of Liberty in Upper New York Bay. However, the island is technically mostly located in New Jersey.

New York City was a major gateway for immigrants in the 18th and 19th centuries. Many were coming from Europe by ship, and New York was one of the closest ports. It was also a booming city with many jobs and diverse neighborhoods of European immigrant populations. It seemed perfect for an immigrant coming from Europe to the United States, which is why so many headed there.

Ellis Island

In the mid to late 19th century, before Ellis Island opened, more than 8 million immigrants were processed in New York City. This indicated a clear need for some sort of processing station. Construction began around 1890, and the first facility on Ellis Island opened on January 1, 1892. That same day, more than 700 immigrants passed through the station, and over the year,

Newly arrived immigrants wait to be processed at Ellis Island in 1921.

nearly 450,000 more were processed there as well. In the first five years, approximately 1.5 million immigrants were processed at Ellis Island.

Exact numbers for the early years are unknown due to a fire that destroyed many records. It broke out on June 15, 1897, and destroyed the buildings on Ellis Island. Two architects, Edward Lippincott Tilton and William A. Boring, were quickly chosen to design new buildings. The newly designed facilities opened in December 1900. It was just in time, since the United States was experiencing a flood of European immigrants, due to the tensions that would soon lead to the outbreak of World War I.

EDWARD LIPPINCOTT TILTON

Edward Lippincott Tilton was no stranger to designing public buildings. Before working on the facilities for Ellis Island with William A. Boring, Tilton was best known for designing nearly 100 libraries in the United States and Canada.

EXCHANGE

BIGGER, BUT STILL NOT ENOUGH!

The new facilities at Ellis Island were much bigger than the original ones. They were designed to process approximately 5,000 immigrants per day, and just the dining hall alone could seat 1,000 people. However, even this was not quite enough. Immigrants were arriving at a record pace in the early 1900s, particularly in 1907, which was the peak year for Ellis Island. On April 17, 1907, officials at Ellis Island processed a staggering 11,747 immigrants. Over the course of 1907, Ellis Island received a total of 1,004,756 immigrants.

IMMIGRATION QUOTAS

There was a brief slowdown in immigration around World War I, but it picked up again in 1921, when 560,971 immigrants were processed at Ellis Island. By this time, Congress had passed the Emergency Quota Act, which limited the number of people of any given nationality that were allowed to enter the United States. Now it was not simply a matter of rubber-stamping immigrants. Immigration officials had to keep track of how many people from any given country were arriving and ensure that the quotas were not exceeded.

The quotas were actually reduced by law, with the passage of the Immigration Act of 1924. It ordered that the yearly number of immigrants from any given country could not exceed 2 percent of the total number of people from that country who were already living in the United States (it had been 3 percent under the Emergency Quota Act).

 Immigrants from Europe often had to wait in long lines to be processed, such as these immigrants in 1907.

The Immigration Act of 1924 also ruled that the 1890 United States Census be used as the basis on which immigration numbers would be calculated. The Emergency Quota Act had used the 1910 Census as its basis. So many immigrants had come to the United States between 1890 and 1910 that using the 1890 Census as a basis for calculation significantly lowered the number of immigrants allowed in. While more than a million immigrants passed through Ellis Island in 1907, quotas lowered that number to a maximum of 164,000 in 1924.

The Immigration Act of 1924 also banned the immigration of Arabs and people from Asia, and significantly restricted the number of African immigrants allowed into the country. According to the United States Office of the Historian, the purpose of the Immigration Act of 1924 was to "preserve the ideal of U.S. homogeneity."

IMMIGRATION FOR ALL?

Homogeneity was what many Americans wanted. They were fine with the idea of the United States being a "melting pot" of cultures—as long as the cultures all melted together into one homogenous American culture. Many Americans were suspicious of immigrants who kept their own customs, language, and traditions even after moving to the United States. Since it set quotas based on existing population, the Immigration Act of 1924 had the effect of strongly favoring European immigrants. At the same time, it sought to keep out people who looked or acted significantly different from the majority of Americans.

ELLIS ISLAND ADAPTS

Due to these changes to immigration law, Ellis Island altered their operations somewhat. It had originally been a sort of haven for immigrants—their first stop on the way to a better life. It put into action words that were engraved on a plaque at the base of the Statue of Liberty's pedestal. The poem, written by Emma Lazarus in 1883, expressed the idea that immigrants were welcome with its reference to "your tired, your poor, your huddled masses."

Immigrants who were refused entry to the United States had to wait for passage back to their home country.

As noble as these sentiments were, the situation changed as immigration policy changed. Ellis Island became less of a processing center and more a detention center. It was a holding place for people to be deported back to their home country if they attempted to enter illegally or in some way violated the terms of their admittance to the United States. During World War II, Ellis Island moved even more away from immigration processing. It became primarily a detention center for those considered a threat to national security or inadmissible to the United States. By 1946, there were so many detainees at Ellis Island that all immigration functions had to be moved to Manhattan. By 1954, Ellis Island was permanently closed. It reopened in 1990 as a museum showcasing the history of immigration to the United States.

Angel Island

While the East Coast had Ellis Island, the West Coast had Angel Island. Its history isn't a particularly pleasant one, though. When gold was discovered in California in 1848, Chinese immigrants began coming to the West Coast. In the next few years, approximately 25,000 flooded the area, and they were not welcomed with open arms. Many worked in the gold mines or prospecting, but when they were pushed out of that work because of racial discrimination, they began taking jobs for the railroad.

Angel Island was the gateway to the West Coast for immigrants from Asia.

Railroad Work

Officials for the Central Pacific Railroad soon
discovered that the Chinese immigrants had a
solid work ethic and were considerably more
reliable than other immigrants they had hired. In
particular, the railroad officials had a poor view
of Irish immigrants, who they thought were lazy and prone to drinking and
fighting. In contrast, the Chinese did their job without much fuss and were
willing to work for lower wages than others.

Chinese immigrants did
much of the backbreaking
labor involved in building
the Transcontinental
Railroad.

Viewed with Suspicion

Those Chinese immigrants who didn't work on the railroad worked at
other low-paying jobs, such as working in shrimp and abalone fisheries.
In general, they found it difficult to gain acceptance by the native-born
population, who recognized their language, culture, and different-colored
skin as foreign.

In the decades that followed, Americans didn't become any more welcoming to Asian immigrants. Legislation was passed to bar them from entering the United States. For example, the Page Act of 1875 barred Asian immigrants from coming to the United States for forced labor jobs and also barred most Chinese women. In 1882, Congress passed the Chinese Exclusion Act, which banned all immigration of Chinese laborers.

Labor unions followed this up in 1905 by creating the Asiatic Exclusion League. This organization was designed to prevent people from emigrating from other countries in Asia, not just China. It was formed in San Francisco, and right around that same time, construction began on a detention center on Angel Island in San Francisco Bay. The center was opened in 1910 and processed immigrants arriving from dozens of countries—including many from China, Japan, Russia, and South Asia.

BEAUTY AMIDST THE SORROW

Despite its breathtaking location in San Francisco Bay, Angel Island was not exactly a happy place. Many immigrants who arrived there were not wanted in the United States, and they were detained for weeks or months while officials sorted out whether their paperwork was valid and whether they should be granted entry into the United States.

The Island was isolated, and there was little to do. Some of the detainees took to writing poetry to pass the time, and they scratched their poems into the walls of the detention center. More than two hundred poems have been recovered and restored. They are now on display at Angel Island, which has become a California State Park.

KANE MINETA

One Angel Island immigrant who was granted entry into the United States went on to have a famous son. Norman Mineta, U.S. Congressman and the first Asian American to serve in a presidential cabinet (under President Bill Clinton), was the fifth and youngest child of Kane and Kunisaku Mineta.

Kunisaku had come to the United States from Japan in 1902 and worked in various factory and farming positions around Salinas, California. In 1907, President Theodore Roosevelt and the government of Japan reached an agreement that allowed Japanese Americans living in

Norman Mineta is shown here in 2014 with the Asian American historian Connie Young Yu.

the United States to bring over their family from Japan. To take advantage of this development, unmarried Japanese American men wanting to start a family would have family or friends back in Japan set up a marriage with a Japanese woman. They would send a picture of themselves to be the groom at the wedding, while never leaving the United States. After the ceremony, they would send for their new bride—called a "picture bride."

Kane Mineta was a picture bride, and she joined her husband after passing through Angel Island in 1914. Immigration officials insisted that the two be married by the State of California before they would allow Kane in, so the two were married in San Francisco the same day Kane arrived.

SENT BACK

Ellis Island was a processing station for immigrants, and Angel Island was technically a processing station too—but in reality, it was more of a detention center. Its purpose was to keep immigrants from China and other Asian nations out of the United States. Immigrants coming into Angel Island were given a physical exam to ensure that they were healthy. If they were not, they were immediately deported. They were also interrogated about their lineage to determine whether they indeed had a right to come into the United States. The interrogation and research into their claimed background could take weeks, months, or in rare cases more than a year. During that time, the immigrants stayed at the detention center.

Angel Island remained a processing and detention center until 1940, when a fire destroyed the administration building. After that time, the services were moved to the mainland, in San Francisco. But in its 30 years as a processing and detention center, Angel Island saw nearly a million immigrants pass through or be deported back to their home country.

Many Chinese immigrants settled in San Francisco, including these in Ross Alley.

CHAPTER 5

TERRITORIES AND INTERNATIONAL WATERS

The two main borders in the United States are the United States–Mexico border and the United States–Canada border, however, they are not the country's only international borders. The United States has two long coasts—one in the east and one in the west—that have ports of entry and different maritime limits and boundaries. Also, the United States has a number of territories (mainly islands) in different parts of the world.

OCEAN JURISDICTION

United States territory does not end where U.S. soil ends. If it did, someone could simply commit a crime in a coastal area, hop on a boat, and immediately be untouchable, out of U.S. jurisdiction. In general, the Law of the Sea treaty, which came into force in 1994, states that there is an area of sea around a body of land that is considered to be under the jurisdiction of that land. It extends for 12 nautical miles (22 km) from the coast.

THE LAW OF THE SEA

The Law of the Sea was actually created more for environmental reasons than legal reasons. In the early 20th century, people began to realize the value of the seas and oceans. There were mineral resources they could use, and fish and other sea life they could harvest. They wanted to use some of these resources, but they also wanted to protect them. Before the Law of the Sea, there was a widely accepted concept that suggested a nation's rights extended 3 nautical miles (5.5 km) out to sea.

Eventually, the United Nations drafted the Convention on the Law of the Sea, and new regulations were established. They extended nations' jurisdiction out to 12 nautical miles (22 km) offshore, and also established guidelines for the protection and management of natural resources in the sea.

Fishing boats must make sure not to stray over maritime boundaries, into another country's territory.

Maritime Boundaries

The United States has maritime boundaries with some countries. For example, the Russia–United States maritime boundary was established as part of the 1990 USA/USSR Maritime Boundary Agreement (although technically it has never been approved by Russia). Russia and Alaska are actually quite close to each other in a couple of places in the Bering Sea, and both of them have a number of islands in their coastal regions. The United States originally purchased Alaska from Russia, and so to determine which islands or land masses belonged to which nation, the two nations established a maritime boundary that generally follows the International Date Line.

LAW ENFORCEMENT ON THE SEAS

If U.S. jurisdiction extends 12 nautical miles (22 km) out to sea, who patrols that region? This responsibility falls to the United States Coast Guard. In fact, they also have jurisdiction in international waters, so their service does not end when they pass the 12-mile point.

Like the agencies that control immigration and Border Patrol on land, the United States Coast Guard operates under the umbrella of the Department of Homeland Security—at least during peacetime. During World War I and World War II, the Coast Guard was overseen by the U.S. Department of the Navy, but it is generally overseen by the Department of Homeland Security.

The United States Coast Guard patrols waterways such as New York Harbor.

THE "THIRD BORDER"

Some consider the Caribbean Sea to be the United States' third border. That's because a significant chunk of America's trade comes through the Caribbean. This has proven to be somewhat problematic, since the Caribbean is made up of small islands that have differing (and sometimes unstable) political systems, such as in Cuba. It also has a mix of different cultures—some stricken by extreme poverty, like Haiti.

Poverty and overcrowding in Port-au-Prince, Haiti, make immigrating to the United States an attractive prospect.

Every bit of unrest and difficulty in this third border region presents a threat to American security and a challenge to it as a border for American trade. To help strengthen this third border region, the government under George W. Bush committed to a Third Border Initiative. It aimed to help cut down on illegal drug trafficking, financial crime, and migrant smuggling in the region, and also support health and security initiatives in the region. The idea was that strengthening the region could only be good for the United States, since they were so reliant on the region for trade.

U.S. TERRITORIES

In addition to the 50 states, the United States has a number of territories. Territories were a common way of organizing land when the United States was still growing. For example, before 1803 the Northwest Territory was an area covering what would eventually become six United States including and around Ohio. The Southwest Territory, covering an area roughly around Tennessee, existed until 1796, when Tennessee was added as a U.S. state. The Alaska Territory existed until 1959, when Alaska was granted statehood. The Hawaii Territory also existed until 1959, when Hawaii became the 50th state.

NEW STATES

In total, as the United States was being formed, 31 territories applied for statehood, and all were granted. In all of those cases, it was intended that the territories would eventually be granted statehood—and indeed they were. However, the United States has also claimed territories for which it has no plans for statehood.

CURRENT U.S. TERRITORIES

Eleven of these territories have no permanent residents—they are simply small islands in the Caribbean Sea and Pacific Ocean that have no native populations. These territories include Palmyra Atoll, Baker Island, Howland Island, Jarvis Island, Johnston Atoll, Kingman Reef, Midway Islands, Bajo Nuevo Bank, Navassa Island, Serranilla Bank, and Wake Island.

The Mexican island of Roca Partida is still covered in guano.

A STAKE IN EXCREMENT

All of the 11 uninhabited United States territories were claimed under the Guano Islands Act of 1856. This act allowed the government to take possession of any unclaimed islands that were found to have guano on them. What is guano? In a word: feces. Guano is excrement from bats, seals, or seabirds. Wondering why the United States wants poop-covered islands? It turns out that guano contains substances that can be used in gunpowder and fertilizer. It was highly sought after in the 1850s, which led Congress to pass the Guano Islands Act so they could ensure a consistent supply of guano.

INHABITED TERRITORIES

At the moment, the United States has five territories with permanent inhabitants. They are Puerto Rico, Guam, the Northern Mariana Islands, the U.S. Virgin Islands, and American Samoa. All five of these territories are unincorporated, along with 10 of the uninhabited territories. The only one of the 16 territories that is incorporated—which, in this case, means part of the United States proper and subject to the laws in the United States Constitution—is the Palmyra Atoll.

THE PALMYRA ATOLL

An atoll is a reef, island, or chain of islands made of coral. The Palmyra Atoll is located in Polynesia, about 1,000 miles (1,609 km) south of Hawaii. It's an archipelago of approximately 50 small islands that make up a total land area of a little over 1.5 square miles (4 sq km). The United States gained the Palmyra Atoll when they acquired the Hawaii Republic in 1898. For whatever reason, when the United States granted Hawaii statehood in 1959, they chose not to include the Palmyra Atoll, so it remains an incorporated territory.

The only people on Palmyra Atoll are temporary residents doing scientific research or government work.

TERRITORIAL GOVERNMENT

Regardless of whether a territory is incorporated or not, all of them are overseen by the United States federal government. However, that does not mean they follow all of the same rules and regulations. The five inhabited territories are self-governing. They have locally elected officials and legislatures. Each one also sends a member to Washington, D.C. to sit in the U.S. House of Representatives, although that member does not have a vote in House issues.

THE BEST-KNOWN TERRITORY?

Although the United States claims to have five territories with permanent inhabitants, you could say that it really has six. The best-known U.S. territory is Washington, D.C.! Technically Washington, D.C. is a district, but it's similar to a territory in that it's part of the United States, but it is not officially a state and it does not have a state government. Washington, D.C. is a federal district under the jurisdiction of Congress. It has been permanently designated as the seat of the U.S. government.

The soaring dome of the United States Capitol graces the skyline of Washington, D.C.

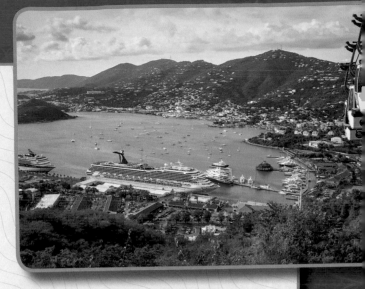

CITIZENSHIP IN THE TERRITORIES

Although the territories function mostly independently of the United States, they are still overseen by the federal government. What that means for citizenship depends on the territory in question. The rules are the same for any person born in Guam, the Northern Mariana Islands, the U.S. Virgin Islands, or Puerto Rico—they are automatically granted U.S. citizenship at birth, just as any person born in the 50 United States is. Only American Samoa has different rules, and people born there become U.S. nationals, not U.S. citizens.

The U.S. Virgin Islands are frequently visited by tourists, including many who arrive by cruise ship.

The reason citizenship rules are different in American Samoa is because of court decisions from the early 20th century. These decisions were called the Insular Cases, and they had to do with what the court saw as incorporated territories and unincorporated territories. Newly acquired territories such as the land around Arizona and New Mexico were incorporated and intended for statehood, but outlying territories like American Samoa were unincorporated, and the courts ruled that people born in Samoa were of an "uncivilized race" and should not be granted citizenship.

FORMER TERRITORIES

Some United States territories have neither gone on to statehood nor remained territories. Some have gone on to become independent countries. Major ones include the Philippines, Micronesia, the Marshall Islands, and Palau.

Court Rulings

The other four inhabited territories are also unincorporated, but court cases over the past century have overturned the rulings in the Insular Cases, declaring them unconstitutional. As a result, people born in those four territories now automatically have American citizenship. For whatever reason, the Insular Case rulings have been upheld when challenged by American Samoans, and so American Samoans are still classified as noncitizen nationals.

This means they cannot be hired for many government jobs, they cannot vote, and in many places they cannot own firearms. American Samoans can apply for United States citizenship, but they must leave American Samoa to do so. Since the citizenship process can take years, most American Samoans cannot just uproot their lives and live somewhere else while waiting to be naturalized.

Challenging the Law

The Obama Administration was criticized for upholding the Insular Cases and denying American Samoans birthright citizenship. Interestingly, though, it may not all have been one-sided. Nine individuals born in American Samoa, as well as the Samoan Federation of America, filed a lawsuit challenging the ruling that people born in American Samoa are not automatically granted U.S. citizenship. As the case worked its way through the United States court system, the government of American Samoa issued a brief that stated that granting birthright citizenship would actually be a threat to Samoa's cultural autonomy.

The Samoan government worried that granting birthright citizenship would be problematic when taken alongside a communal land policy in Samoa. This policy stated that communally owned land can be sold only to a person who has at least 50 percent Samoan ancestry. So at this point, the law still stands. If a person is born in a territory other than American Samoa, they have United States citizenship from birth.

 An immigrant from American Samoa enjoys the sun in Garden Grove, California.

» THE MAN BEHIND THE SAMOAN LAWSUIT

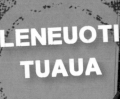

LENEUOTI TUAUA

Leneuoti Tuaua is an American Samoan and a noncitizen national. In 2012, he filed a lawsuit against the State Department and the Obama administration on the grounds that the Fourteenth Amendment to the Constitution grants automatic citizenship to people born in the United States. The case made its way up to the Supreme Court, but in June 2016, the Supreme Court declined to hear it and the case was dropped. Several of Tuaua's co-plaintiffs in the case had served in the U.S. military, so they were seen as being fit for service—but not for citizenship.

CHAPTER 6

BUILDING THE WALL

One of the most memorable parts of the 2016 presidential race was Republican presidential nominee Donald Trump's repeated claim that if elected, the United States would build a wall between the U.S. and Mexico—and get Mexico to pay for it. On November 8, 2016, Donald Trump was elected as the nation's 45th president, and now the United States waits to see whether he will follow through on his promise to build the wall.

WHY A WALL?

It is an indisputable fact that there are indeed many immigrants living in the United States who have entered the country illegally—and many have done so by crossing the United States–Mexico border. As part of Trump's campaign, he promised to take a stand on the number of undocumented immigrants coming into the United States. One way of doing this was to step up efforts to find and deport undocumented immigrants—and he has already issued executive orders to try to make this happen.

Another way of addressing the problem of immigration, in Trump's view, was to build a physical, impenetrable wall along the nearly 2,000 miles (3,219 km) of the border between the United States and Mexico. This proposal struck a chord with Trump's supporters, who began to chant "Build the wall!" at the rallies Trump held during the 2016 campaign. Perhaps not surprisingly, one of Trump's first actions after assuming the office of president was to issue an executive order directing that the construction of the wall should begin immediately.

HOW MUCH WILL IT COST?

It's hard to know exactly how much it would cost to build the wall until the actual construction gets underway. Many Trump supporters feel that the cost is irrelevant, because they believe that Trump will carry through on his promise to make Mexico pay for the wall. However, a 2017 report from the Department of Homeland Security estimated the cost of construction at $22 billion. That number is almost twice as much as the $12 billion Trump claimed the wall would cost when he discussed it during his campaign. The likely reason for the increase is that the official Department of Homeland Security estimate includes the costs the government will have to pay to acquire the private lands the wall will be constructed on.

Building a wall across inhospitable desert terrain will be an enormous undertaking.

WHO'S GOING TO PAY?

Another surprising part of Trump's proposal to build a wall was his insistence that Mexico would pay for the construction of it. Many people wondered why Mexico would willingly pay for a wall that was not their idea in the first place.

Apparently Mexican President Enrique Peña Nieto wondered the same thing. Just days after Trump took office and began moving forward with the wall, President Nieto stated, "Mexico does not believe in walls. I've said time again; Mexico will not pay for any wall." Nieto's predecessor, Vicente Fox, was not quite as polite and used colorful language when responding to the idea that Mexico would pay for the wall.

The idea of having Mexico pay, though, isn't as outlandish as it might seem. It might just be a bit indirect. The Trump administration is reportedly considering implementing a tax on imports coming through Mexico that would yield billions of dollars in tax revenue for the United States. That tax revenue could then be spent to build the wall.

POTENTIAL CHALLENGES

A major challenge to building Trump's proposed wall is, of course, the cost. Spending $22 billion on the construction of this border wall is a significant amount of money, even for a federal government, and it remains to be seen whether the United States government will actually get Mexico to finance the project.

But there are other challenges, too. When George W. Bush was president and attempted to build several hundred miles of fencing along portions of the border, the government ran into numerous problems. One of these problems included that not all private landowners were willing to have a large fence constructed on their property. The government offered these landowners buyouts, but not all of them were interested.

Another challenge is the Rio Grande, which defines the border in Texas. A 1970 treaty dictated that structures built along the border could not disrupt the flow of the river. That treaty is still in effect. Because the flow of the river can change, particularly during times of heavy rainfall or flooding, that means any wall would have to be constructed well away from the river. In some areas, the wall would have to be constructed a fair distance into the United States, on property privately owned or, in one case, owned by a Native American tribe.

President George W. Bush suggested building a similar wall, but ran into significant challenges.

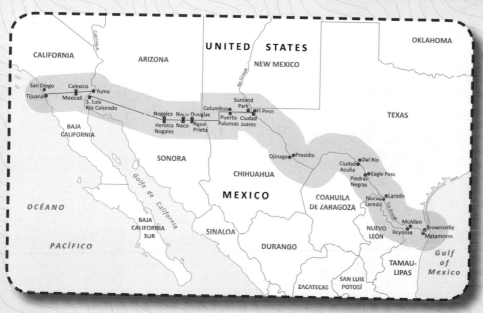

 This map shows some of the many cities—on both sides of the border—that the wall would pass through.

OTHER CONCERNS

Aside from the issues involved in trying to secure rights to the privately owned or Native American-owned lands, there's another problem. If the wall is constructed well into the United States, a fair distance away from the river, the strip of land between the river and the wall then becomes a sort of no-man's-land. It would technically be U.S. land, but the United States would find it hard to effectively police land that's behind a large wall.

There are other environmental concerns that come along with the idea of building a wall. The border in Southern California runs partly along some sand dunes, which, like the river, can shift depending on the weather. For environmental reasons, the government is not allowed to build any structure that would impede the movement of the dunes, so they would instead have to construct a sort of floating wall in that region.

The government would also have to take measures to ensure the protection of the dozens of federally protected species of wildlife that live along the California and Arizona portions of the border.

REASONS FOR BUILDING THE WALL

With all of these challenges to constructing the proposed wall, one might wonder why the Trump administration is even bothering to pursue it. First and foremost, of course, is the fact that people who support the construction of the wall truly believe it will help combat the problem of illegal border crossings. And indeed, it most likely will help limit the number of people who cross illegally.

In Winterhaven, California, a road dead-ends at the border with Mexico.

Currently, there are unprotected sections of the border where people can simply walk or swim across, and no one notices. They are dangerous areas (due to environmental conditions), and people do die trying to cross, but it can be done. And if an impenetrable wall were constructed along those areas, it's far less likely that people would be able to simply cross.

Supporters of the idea of the wall point out other positive aspects, too. Some point out that the wall will create jobs. Many laborers will be needed to help construct the wall, and workers will be needed to maintain it after it's built. Some also point out that the materials used to build the wall can be obtained from U.S. companies, which would provide a temporary boost to those companies.

MORE BENEFITS

Others point out that the people who own private land on which the wall is constructed will earn money by allowing the government to purchase or use their land. In addition, to construct the wall, the government will have to build roads to some previously unaccessible places, which could be useful for other purposes.

Many of these arguments relate to temporary benefits—for example, jobs that will exist while the wall is being constructed, and payouts that are given to landowners when the wall is built. But a longer-term benefit that many people propose is that the wall could help stem the flow of illegal drugs being transported over the border. Just as people would have a much harder time crossing over a wall, in theory so would drugs.

WILL IT WORK?

Ultimately, the question is whether a wall would work. Some believe it would, citing the Berlin Wall, which effectively separated East and West Berlin for decades before being knocked down in 1989. Further back in history, the Great Wall of China protected the Chinese empire from numerous outside groups.

 Whether the wall is built or not, border crossings and checkpoints will continue to be crowded with people waiting to cross.

Others disagree, though, saying that if people want to cross a border badly enough, they will find a way. Ruben Andersson, a London anthropologist and author of *Illegality, Inc.: Clandestine Migration and the Business of Bordering Europe*, spoke about current border fences in European countries. He said, "These fences are not solving anything. Numbers are not going down. People will find a way. Fences also generate novel and more dramatic entry methods, such as the collective 'runs' at the fences we have seen at various borders in recent years."

THE FUTURE OF THE BORDERS

In some ways, the future of the borders looks stable. The United States has already acquired all of the continental land mass it is likely to for the foreseeable future. That means that the borders with Canada and Mexico are unlikely to change substantially—although the look of the United States–Mexico border will certainly be altered if the wall is constructed as proposed.

Protesters in Portland, Oregon, oppose President Trump's border wall and immigration bans.

However, the enforcement of those borders is facing a period of change. Those changes depend on what the Trump administration and the administrations that follow decide to do in terms of immigration policy and law. The only thing certain is that border debates and discussions are unlikely to go away, given that Americans have strong and differing ideas on the value and role of immigrants in the country.

GLOSSARY

49th parallel A circle of latitude 49 degrees north of the equator. Part of the 49th parallel delineates a section of the United States–Canada border.

archipelago A group of islands.

asylee A person who is seeking or granted political asylum.

asylum Protection granted to someone who has left their home country due to political strife.

autonomy The right to self-govern.

communal Shared between people. Work and property can both be communal.

contiguous Next to or touching; sharing a common border.

cybercrime A criminal activity carried out on the Internet.

flash flooding Sudden, localized flooding, usually brought on by heavy rains.

forced labor Work that people are forced to do under the threat of punishment.

Great Lakes Five large interconnected lakes in North America.

homogeneity The state of all being the same or similar.

human trafficking The trade of humans, usually for forced labor.

International Date Line An imaginary line running from the North Pole to the South Pole, roughly along the 180 degree line of longitude.

jurisdiction Official power to make legal decisions and judgments.

lineage Descent through ancestry.

Louisiana Purchase The acquisition of 828,000 square miles (2.14 million sq km) of land from France in 1803. The parcel stretched through the Midwest, all the way from the Canadian border to the Gulf of Mexico.

money laundering The process of making money obtained illegally appear to be legal.

noncitizen national A person born in American Samoa or Swains Island who does not have a parent who is an American citizen.

Polynesia An area of more than 1,000 islands in the central and southern Pacific Ocean. Hawaii, New Zealand, and Easter Island roughly form the edges of Polynesia.

port of entry An area, such as a harbor or airport, through which people or products can enter a country.

precursor A person or thing that came before another.

refugee A person forced to leave their home country to escape political strife, natural disaster, or persecution.

temperate Mild.

tribunal A court of justice.

undercurrent A collective underlying feeling.

unincorporated Not included as part of a whole.

whirlpool A rapidly rotating body of water that can draw objects into it.

work ethic The idea that hard work is its own reward.

FOR MORE INFORMATION

BOOKS

Currie, Stephen. *Undocumented Immigrant Youth*. San Diego, CA: ReferencePoint Press, 2017.

McCormick, Lisa Wade. *Frequently Asked Questions About Growing Up as an Undocumented Immigrant*. New York: Rosen Classroom, 2012.

Saldana Jr., Rene. *Juventud! Growing Up on the Border: Stories and Poems*. VAO Publishing, 2013.

Weir, William. *Border Patrol*. New York: Chelsea House Publishing, 2011.

WEBSITES

To learn more about U.S. borders, visit the U.S. Customs and Border Protection site.
www.cbp.gov/border-security/along-us-borders/overview

The Library of Congress's Places in History page has maps relevant to historical events.
www.loc.gov/rr/geogmap/placesinhistory

This website provides information about the Louisiana Purchase and the expansion of the United States.
www.loc.gov/collections/louisiana-european-explorations-and-the-louisiana-purchase/about-this-collection/

INDEX